ALL IN

D'MARIO D. CARTER

ALL IN

D'Mario D. Carter

Cover Art:
Dominic D. Harris
CEO of 1 of 3 Stooges Design

ISBN: 9781980632696

For more information about D'Mario's upcoming
events and projects, please visit the following
links.

www.dmariocarter.com

www.instagram.com/wokeandheard

This book is dedicated to all those who have contributed to the person I am today. Whether it was positive or negative, thank you for your impact. It has molded me into a solid.

Table Of Contents

THE BOY   6

THE ADOLESCENT   35

THE MAN   66

ME   114

THE BOY

All In

There is no award for giving up

Achieve what you must

Success is something not a lot of people touch

So I'm going to put it in a headlock

And never let it go

And leave no doubt

I'm going to give my all

No shortcuts no bowing out

No tap out no surrender

Achievement is a goal that is on each day of my agenda

When people work hard they say they need time off or rest

But I'm working hard over here

Trying to buy my mom a house

And write in amounts she needs on blank checks

I will never settle for less

I'm not a simple dude that only wants the chips

Give me the

Guacamole

Salsa

Sour cream

Cheese

And the dip

People say

"Dang D you've changed"

No

I just went from four quarters to a dollar

No more loose change

To know me you know my struggle

To know me you know my pain

You wouldn't feel my heart

If my blood was running through your veins

Who are you to tell me what I can and can't do

I play tag with ambition

Kick it with motivation

And dismiss all that adolescent hatred

Everything I went through was for a purpose

I am who I am today because of it

All of it

Every individual thing

From the gun in my face

To totaling my car

And my mother's close encounter with death

Had me talking to myself

Like *damn what the hell is next*

See this is the good

The bad and the scary

At times I had to crawl because my legs got too weary

My trials are my foundation

I'm a human being standing taller than any structural creation

They say you can't take a nigga out the hood

Unless he's going to jail

Well my university was my institution

Tuition well call that bail

And the dorm is the closest I ever got to a cell

Only difference is

I'm not a nigga

I'm a young black male

-    **The Boy**

Home

I grew up on 45th and Othello

Located in the Southend of Seattle

SoufEnd with an "F" if you're from there

I learned how to shoot a gun before I knew how to tie a tie

I knew how to play hide and go seek

With bullets entering my home without a knock

I have seen more sparks on the block

Than I have seen in the sky on the 4th of July

I learned how to shoot a gun before I knew how to tie a tie

-    **The Boy**

Winners Circle

On your mark

Get set

Go

The race began

But my heart was stuck in the blocks

You never noticed

Your focus was on winning

- **The Boy**

Unseen

I love long walks on the beach at night
I can't see my shadow
It haunts me in the day
And reminds me of who I am

The dark hides my guilt
Protecting me from the monster within

My imperfections have become bad habits
That I cannot break

The night hides my shadow
And serves as the VIP entrance
To my closet full of skeletons

-      **The Boy**

No Air

I'm looking at your lips hoping they stop moving

I'm playing a game of pin the tail on the donkey

But instead of a tail it's my lips vs yours

You stop for a second to take in some air

And I see my window to take your breath away

Once our tongues unlock

You give me the key to your heart

And I present you with a ring of commitment

That is what today is all about

It's about me and you and no one else

You place your palm in my hand

And we will walk down this aisle

As woman and man

There are a lot of fish in the sea

I never knew I would find a mermaid

I was told they didn't exist

Cupid shot me with a poisonous arrow

From an aerial attack

The venom seeped deep into my veins

Up my arm

Poured into my heart and punctured my soul

I've been infected and I don't want a cure

- **The Boy**

Numerical Love

1

2

3

Please don't let me get to 10

No you asked for this

I didn't ask for anything

You wanted me

You got me

4

5

6

I want who I first met

Not this person in front of me

I used to love you with all my heart

We've been together for 10 years

7

8

9

10 is where it started

And 10 is where it will end

- **The Boy**

Eye See

You're so arrogant

Stuck up

Selfish

Full of yourself

Self-centered

Conceited

Cocky

Motivation comes in many forms

Sincerely

Your Reflection

- **The Boy**

Mona Lisa

Don't touch me

Please don't

Every time your fingertips brush across my skin

They paint an ugly picture

All I see is you and him

But you continue to illustrate this image

And I keep allowing it

Because the brush strokes feel so good

So touch me until the picture is a masterpiece

- **The Boy**

24/7

My arms wrap around you

Like hands on a clock

Holding you until the world disappears

I close my eyes

The only thing that is absent is you

Time waits for no man

And neither did you

I open my eyes

And this place I'm in

Is unfamiliar

Last night it was a dwelling full of life

Today I'm in a realm loaded with pain

- **The Boy**

Fear

I used to be afraid of the dark

Then I opened my eyes

It was then I realized the dark was not so scary

What was terrifying

Were the images I saw

Once my eyes were open

Pain

Hurt

Death

The norm

What surprised me was

Reality

- **The Boy**

Truth Prevails

At the end of the storm

It was your true colors

That appeared

Not a rainbow

- **The Boy**

Don't Snooze

Dreams come true

But you must quit dreaming

You can't accomplish anything sleeping

Dreams turn into goals

Goals turn into reality

But first you must

WAKE UP

- **The Boy**

Metro

7

9

42

106

- **The Boy**

True Or False

Answering *"where you from"*

From the older kids on the bus

Made questions on the SAT seem simple

- **The Boy**

90's Nick

I think you are All That

I love you how Kel loves Orange Soda

We are just some Rugrats

But I want to be the Doug Funnie

To your Patty Mayonnaise

- **The Boy**

Death

I don't understand you

You're so sneaky and misleading

You love to hide in the shadows

And you are so damn greedy

Thief

Taking life with no regard

With no intentions of giving it back

Please make me one promise

The day you come for me

Return me back

To all my loved ones

You stole from me

- **The Boy**

Millennial Romance

We argue about Instagram likes

And who we retweet on Twitter

In this relationship for two

Leave me alone

I need Myspace

After seeing that pic with you and Tom

Siri I can't believe you did this to me

I should have dated Alexa

I'm the furthest thing from a Mac

But our Windows of opportunity have closed

Logging off forever

-    **The Boy**

No Appetite

We eat at the table

But won't discuss the starvation in the house

Our communication is a meal that is prepped

But never makes its way out of the kitchen

We remain hungry

While we consume a full-course meal

-   **The Boy**

I Love You like

It's more than that cute puppy love

Eskimo kisses

Note sharing and bear hugs

I love you like

Little kids love stepping on icky bugs

Like doctors love scrubs

Like coffee loves a mug

Like fiends love drugs

I love you like not now but right now

I love you like mom upside down

In other words I love you like wow

I love you like thugs love the ghetto

Like Pinocchio loves Geppetto

Like Cupid loves his arrows

Like roses loves their petals

I love you like I love to play ball

You're the best ref I ever had

Never gave me a bad call

I love you like I love myself

But I'll put you before me

Just to see that smile reach to the other cheek

I love you more than things stated in this poem

But in the end I hope this poem lets it all be known

I love you like how I wish we could restore our history

But that was the past this is a new week

Now the only thing I love

Is how we used to be

-   **The Boy**

Non-Fiction

We are told

Not to judge a book by its cover

But I've been judged by my color

Is my mouth not worthy of speaking

Are you that good

That you can take one glance at me

And know about the biography brewing inside me

More potent than any cup of coffee

You will ever drink

I am an advanced memoir

So innovative

Your mind can't comprehend the cover

- **The Boy**

A Son's View (Dedicated to Mama Peaches)

I used to think it was hard being a child

Getting told what to do

No dessert before dinner

And having to be in the house by a given time

To make curfew

Us boys could not wait to be grown

But even as an adult mom still wants you to come home

It wasn't hard being a kid

Our minds just couldn't grasp the unconditional love

That was produced from our mother's hearts

And showered onto our souls

As a child you never thought to stop

It was always

"Ok mom I got to go"

We were outside until the sun fell asleep

But made sure we were in the house well before

The streetlights awakened from their slumber

The aroma of mama's home cooked meals

Could seduce any kid

To migrate home

It was the ultimate trap

We never wanted to do wrong

Well…

Not purposely

But you have to understand us boys will be boys

Until we develop into MEN

As a man it's amazing how I finally realize

A woman becoming a mother is more than how life begins

Not only are women mothers

They are

Life providers

Nurturers

Doctors when we are sick

Protectors when we are in trouble

Accountants that manage our funds

And best friends when we need to talk

A mother's love cannot be replaced

It reaches heights even I can't begin to explain

Altitudes that surpass clouds

Stars

Skyscrapers

And planes

Heights that go beyond the moon and outer space

I'm pretty sure God let my mom borrow Orion's Belt

A few times to put me back in my place

As a son all we want to do is make you proud

And not see you struggle

Listen to you cheer for us and try to stay out of trouble

We LOVE our mothers

We consider you our queens

You are the only ones that can raise a prince into a king

- **The Boy**

THE ADOLESCENT

Limbo

Sometimes I call you and hang up

Just hoping that you call back

When we were together my heart beat red with joy

Now its bruised blue and black

And in its place there is a void

I can't be with you because you're tired of this

And sick of that

But I'm frustrated at the fact

That you won't let me get you back

I was never a bad dude

Even when I took them elbows and fist to the face

I still never laid hands on you

I remember the first night that you saw me cry

You said

"Babe are those tears"

I said

"No I'm good and quickly dried my eyes"

Now when I cry there's no one beside where I lie

You probably don't care but that's just FYI

I know I'm not perfect

I got a past that comes with my present

But I tried to change for you

I put you first and me second

- **The Adolescent**

Growth

My roots run deep

My ancestors were entangled within trees

To start a foundation for me

- **The Adolescent**

Point Blank Range

Goosebumps painted my body

Creating a picture

Picasso himself could not create

Passion discharged from my soul

You are envisioning art

But I saw my life flashing before my eyes

All these colors

But Black is always the focus

Officer

"*FREEZE*"

But Officer…

(Draws Gun)

"*STOP TALKING*"

I was posing for a photo

Knees rooted into the cement

Hands interlocked behind my head

Praying to God the photographer didn't shoot

- **The Adolescent**

Bull's-Eye

I'm a target

I never asked for this role

But it is one that has been forced upon me

Since birth I have been looked at differently

I've gone from an innocent baby

To a child

And somehow developed into a threat

Now I walk down the street with a bullseye on my chest

- **The Adolescent**

Sentiment

Compassion is not taught

It is located in the same place as love

Let your guard down

These superficial barriers won't endure

Let your heart feel what your eyes see

Allow your soul to cry

It's ok to be human

- **The Adolescent**

Willpower

No

We are not acting like victims

We are fed up

We are speaking out

We will not remain silent

We will organize

We will exist

We will fight

We will be heard

Even when they won't let us speak

We will survive

Even when they don't want us to live

We will...

-   **The Adolescent**

Face The Facts

Stop using the American flag as a blindfold

To hide from the truth

Wake up

If you can't see the injustices

If you can't recognize the racism

If you can't feel the pain

Then take the blindfold off

The flag is not the focus

Kneeling during the anthem isn't the problem

The issue lies within society

And the ignorance in our justice system

-   **The Adolescent**

Bloody Shoes

I wanted to be your happily ever after

Even though life is far from a fairytale

I would have fought dragons for you

Defeated Witches Goblins and Goons

Damn a glass slipper

I would have brought you back red bottoms

So I could follow your path of destruction

And never forget how you broke my heart

- **The Adolescent**

Poor Connection

Our communication is equivalent

To dial up internet

And to be honest

I'm tired of waiting

This relationship has been loading for years

Somehow we are still at 50 percent

- **The Adolescent**

Nice Weather

A raindrop fell on my head

It was so odd

Because it was the middle of June

In Los Angeles

There wasn't a cloud in the sky

But I never thought to look up

At the flash flood that was drowning your face

- **The Adolescent**

Corporate America

Please provide

A minimum of five years experience

Three references

A copy of your resume

And a cover letter

Privilege

Also accepted

- **The Adolescent**

Question

How can you defend yourself
In a country that won't fight for you

- **The Adolescent**

Crayola

Color brings things to life

Turns pictures into masterpieces

Paints the faces of our world

Racism will never see true beauty

Just a colorless one-dimensional boring ass view

- **The Adolescent**

People

You can't consider yourself

A homophobe if you eat Skittles

You've been tasting the rainbow

- **The Adolescent**

Demolished

I was so attracted to your mind

Until our foundation became weak

Your thoughts became fragile

And we became broken

- **The Adolescent**

Hello

My hand will tell you

The first five things you need to know about me

All you have to do

Is

Hold it

- **The Adolescent**

Loan

Since you're not going to use it

Can I borrow your privilege

- **The Adolescent**

Endure

As I sunk to the bottom

I did not say a word

So you could still brag about me

To your shallow friends

- **The Adolescent**

Seasons

Summer turns into fall

But we are stuck in the same place

My favorite time of the year is you

Why can't we progress together

Why do the seasons change

But we remain stagnant

Maybe we need a change of scenery

I hear California is nice year-round

- **The Adolescent**

Typical "*Black*" Week

Monday - Thursday

Black male

Friday - Saturday

Criminal

Sunday

John Doe

- **The Adolescent**

Love Recipient

I adore seeing your name

Appear on the screen of my phone

I get excited like a kid

On Christmas Eve night

I hate group chats

But for you

I would create one and add ten different numbers

That all contact you

This way when you text me

Your name would show as many times

As my heart skips beats

-    **The Adolescent**

Independent

When they become heartless

Show no emotion

Display no interest

Remind yourself

Who loves you

- **The Adolescent**

What If

At the end of the day

It was her laugh

The suffering in her eyes

And our depth filled conversations

That made me question everything

But our hearts never communicated

- **The Adolescent**

Geometry

I don't know what to say

Or what to do

I continue to turn in circles

Finding myself back at square one

-    **The Adolescent**

The Beauty Of Depth

My skin is external

A cover to a book you may never read

You see my surface

But can you comprehend my soul

- **The Adolescent**

Perception

The ungrateful

Will plant seeds

Return to a forest

Full of trees

But complain about

Their seeds being gone

- **The Adolescent**

Honor The Journey

The pursuit of happiness

Does not come without

A trail of struggle

Do not glorify my success

Without acknowledging

My beautiful trials

- **The Adolescent**

BLM

I never knew

Wearing a hoodie was a crime

I never knew

Skittles could be used as a deadly weapon

I never knew

Black lives mattered

Please excuse my confusion

I've seen groups in white hooded robes never get shot

So I thought hoodies were socially acceptable

I've seen people of all races taste the rainbow

And not be considered a threat

So I thought Skittles were just candy

I never knew I had to tell you specifically my life mattered

Because it was a black one

I thought that was implied

It's crazy

Black lives only matter

After

We

DIE

- **The Adolescent**

THE MAN

Live Life

Regret is one hell of a hangover

- **The Man**

We Are One (Well... we should be)

Hate is taught

Love is given

Respect is earned

Color is a description

Race is an event

Equality

Is for EVERYONE

-    **The Man**

Sobriety Test

The truth in your voice

Faded quicker than my buzz

I hate you when I'm sober

- **The Man**

IG

I'm so addicted to you

I can't live a day without you

Your color

Content

Capabilities

And that thick juicy app

My thumb can't wait to double tap

I love to scroll up and down

But I'm sorry I lack the commitment you seek

You're so far from faithful

Everyone you see you let download for free

\-   **The Man**

The Credit Cycle

It's hard to escape a reality

That brings hope

Even if the cost is too high

Money can't buy happiness

But debt can

We purchase material things

That we cannot afford

Just to provide us with temporary smiles

Smiles that fade into grins

Grins that become frowns

Frowns that become tears

And then…

We purchase again

I continue to swipe

Until my expiration date

Not even debt can defeat death

- **The Man**

Greater Than Rocket Science

It's complicated

The answers are right in front of me

It's difficult to comprehend the problem

When the equation no longer holds value

-    **The Man**

Conclusion

I gave up everything

Just to lose you

You took everything to gain me

Now we blend into the world like camouflaged strangers

Maybe the next time I see you

I'll stop and introduce myself

Hello

My name is…

- **The Man**

Obtuse

All men are created equal

But all eyes don't comprehend

Race

Religion

And

Gender

- **The Man**

Search Committee

If you need me
I'll be looking for
Who you used to be

-    **The Man**

WTF

I told you the truth

But you shut me up

So I began to lie

And you started to listen

- **The Man**

Flared Temper

Anger is one hell of an emotion

At least when lava increases

You know how it will exit the volcano

But you never know how anger will erupt

Or the amount of destruction

It will leave behind

Approach me with caution

I don't want to make you a victim

-    **The Man**

Suffering

Give me the knife

My heart cannot bear

The trauma you would endure

After stabbing me in the back

I've inflicted wounds on myself before

There is no pain

Just this dull feeling of disappointment

- **The Man**

Distractions

When you turn the switch off

On the people who once shined

So bright in your life

Maybe their light began to dim

Or maybe your illumination became brighter

So brilliant they couldn't bare your radiance

Then again

Maybe they were never shining in your life

But they were blinding you from happiness

They're the reason you could never

Open your eyes

-    **The Man**

Perseverance

You have broken me

Paralyzed me with heartache

You have stripped me of my happiness

Disregarded my love

Tormented my feelings

You have turned my days into nights

But I think you forgot

Stars shine brightest in the dark

-   **The Man**

Cold Front

If I could stop time

I would freeze it

Hoping to never have a memory melt away

I would hate to see our history

Flow down the drain

We are solid like ice

What other people see

Is the tip of the iceberg

Only we know our true depth

Most can't weather the storm

But we created a season

Winter

- **The Man**

School Girl

How can you be confused

The solution is right in front of you

I've been the answer key

To your complicated love equation

But you are a good student

With too much pride to cheat

    -   **The Man**

Experience

I woke up from a dream

And entered a nightmare

Life has shown me

No fairytales

I've lived realities

Imaginations could not fathom

- **The Man**

The Depth Of Beauty

A wave is a thing of beauty

Shifting her hips

From one direction to another

Creating curves men would die for

Floating in awe

Not realizing her ability

To take breath away

Caution

Admire from a far

- **The Man**

Another Round

I love Whiskey

So I continue to take shots until I'm tipsy

I love you

You're poison

But I love you

Even though you hurt me

I want every ounce of you

- **The Man**

Love Letters Don't Work

I write

With hopes of one day

Seducing your eyes to focus on paper

That new love fascination

The *what is he doing*

How is he

I haven't talked to him in five minutes

And I already miss him

Type of attraction

At the end of the day

Talk is cheap

But

Words last forever

-      **The Man**

Who Are You

How can I look up to you

You were never a role model to me

The last footsteps I want to follow are yours

I'm told I should talk to you about how I feel

I've been talking for years

Dropping hints and clues

Actions speak louder than words

But you couldn't see those either

- **The Man**

The Reveal

It was a game of peek a boo

Until I was asked to hide my identity

Why must my race be another lost item in the attic

I have never been ashamed of my skin color

My Melanin holds value

More than that new Range Rover

Parked in front of your house

With depreciation soaking into the tires

They bought and sold us way before cars

But our Melanin holds too much worth for a price tag

- **The Man**

Stages

When you're a boy

You think being a man consists of the following

Being tough

Not crying

Instilling dominance

Don't show vulnerability

Act hard

At ALL TIMES

Use violence to get your point across

As a man I learned how wrong society was

Women should be treated like queens

Not objects

I learned that crying is an action that expresses emotion

Tough is just a word

To be vulnerable is to be strong

Save the acting for the professionals

If you can't use your words then are you really a *man*

It is a privilege to have responsibility

So take care of them

- **The Man**

Keep Your Sympathy

You must go through so much pain
Each day
Peering out of the two windows God provided you as eyes
You see things that should have been censored
Why was viewer's discretion never advised
Reality TV makes real life look like a book
Written by Stephen King
You poor thing
The suffering you must endure
This is the truth I live
Do not sympathize me
I do not have the privilege nor the time to do so myself

-    **The Man**

Mind Games

Lost in a river of hopes and dreams

Swept in a current of broken promises and false truths

One does not know they are drowning

Until they start to take in water

Panic begins

And terror takes over the body

I don't want to die here

Do not lie to me anymore

Don't promise me something you cannot provide

I enjoyed floating gently down the stream

Why did you make me alter my path

Now I am in unfamiliar waters

Anxiously searching for shore

-   **The Man**

KP

I did not know what to say

When I picked up my phone

And received the gut-wrenching news

Of you getting murdered

I never knew what to tell your sister or mom

All the words that came to mind

Would not have fit the holes in their chest

Even now

I don't know what to say

I have gotten a few more phone calls

Similar to the one I got about you

They all start off the same

With a "*Hey*"

Weighing heavier than gravity itself

I should have let all the calls go to voicemail

I wonder if I would have called back

The *Do Not Disturb* feature

Couldn't prevent these calls from incoming

-    **The Man**

Growing Pains

We go through this life and accumulate materials

But what about the things we can't see

What about the damage from those ex-lovers

What about your pride that was crushed

So you picked up the pieces

Placed them in your pockets

Right next to your insecurities

What about that internal battle you have with yourself

Every single day

I'm still trying to figure out what the score is to that match

Pretty sure I was up one last time that I checked

I used to drink out the bottle to kill the pain

But 40 proof began to taste like H2O

- **The Man**

Culture

Full-flavored steam

Spewing from the surface of the stove

Crock-Pot full of flavor

A recipe so unique

Imitation holds no substance

And duplication is impossible

-   **The Man**

Credit Check

Homicide rates

Rise quicker than credit scores

But they still focus on the 700+

- **The Man**

Know Your Worth

I saw hope

When I should have been looking for love

See

I had hoped you loved me

I hoped you found me attractive

I hoped I was good enough for you

How dumb of me to look for hope

When love does not hide in the shadows

Love is bright and vivid like a warm spring day

You don't have to question love

Or who loves you

Love is a magnet that connects me and...well

Not you

- **The Man**

Tide Pull

Emotions are like the tide

Constantly pushing and pulling the heart

Similar to how

The tide abuses the shore

Leaving

Just to come back

-       **The Man**

Throw It

The word *love* is thrown around like a frisbee

I heave *love* like a boomerang

Waiting for it to return

With a force

That will knock me on my ass

Fake *love* has no impact

I will know if you mean it

-   **The Man**

DDC

I was born February 19th 1991

A 9lb 9oz baby boy

Labeled by society as a target

As soon as I was considered to be a threat

1991 through 1995 I was cute

1996 through 2000 I was growing

2001 through 2005 beware

2006 through 2010 I made the world nervous

2011 through 2014 I became a target

2015 to the present I became target practice

In the future they don't want me to exist

But they can't kill history

Faith can't be beat

And dreams can't be murdered

My blood

My tears

My sweat

My pain

My heart

My soul

This is my BLACK HISTORY

- **The Man**

Service Provider

I call

But the message never seems to reach you

I continue to leave it after the beep

Somehow you never receive it

I text **IN ALL CAPITAL BOLD LETTERS**

But you still don't get the notification

I verbally tell you in person

I'm watching your eyes read my lips

I wish your ears would catch the words

My soul is spewing out

Why do my messages seem to be *undeliverable*

I'm roaming through life

With a dead zone of bad connections

I guess you're just another one of those service providers

Nothing more

Nothing less

- **The Man**

Adult Content

I want to talk

Until my intellect penetrates your soul

And you wake up in the morning

Confused at the one-night stand

We just had with no physicality

- **The Man**

Flame

Hype

Only offers an initial spark

Fireworks are pretty

But then what...

Provide something that keeps my fuse lit

For eternity

- **The Man**

Juanita Carter

Wake up

Wake up

Why won't you move

Why are you so cold

Granny

I got you a blanket

I hope it provides your soul

With the warmth you provided me in life

You never let me freeze

But without you

I will never

Reach that level of warmth again

- **The Man**

Closed Mouth

Freedom of speech

Right

How is it your opinion holds more value than mine

You have no fear to speak your mind

But I have to strategically map out my sentences

Like I'm taking a damn entrance exam

For an advanced placement class called life

It is so frustrating

But my annoyance comes off as anger

And that becomes the focus

The typical "*angry black man*"

Equipped with a loud voice

A raised fist

And enough melanin

To strike fear into all those

Who do not carry the same burdens as being black

- **The Man**

Is It You

Follow me into the land of the unknown

Our next step could be our last

Or

It could be the first step to the rest of our lives

You're not conservative

Because you took a chance on me

You are brave

Your friends say you're stupid

Running off with a guy you barely know

But they don't know me

Don't let their ignorance blind you

Hopefully I'm your happily ever after

Or the first man to ever make you this happy

-   **The Man**

Ex-Factor

Continue to provide me warmth

Similar to a sunny day

Let your rays shine on me

Naive to the true danger you possess

I continue to bask in your radiance

Harming myself in the process

But you bring me joy

Even if I was to tell you the truth

You would never see tears

Just a sun kissed face

-    **The Man**

Douglas Fir

Your faith sways

Like branches on a tree

You've been broken

One branch after another

Don't give up

Stay grounded

God has given you the strength to survive

You will not be uprooted

- **The Man**

Ta-Dah

The only time you claimed me

Was when success was present

Where were you when struggle entered my life

This whole time I thought magic was fake

Unaware of the master magician in my presence

I guarantee you

Your disappearing act

Will be one to remember

Too bad I won't be there to watch

- **The Man**

Rejected

They say don't forget where you came from

But that has never been a problem for me

The focus point should be

My existence

Because that keeps getting denied

-    **The Man**

Imposter

I saw you the other day

You were standing

Right next to the guilt you've been avoiding

You are a poacher

I witnessed you murder the elephant in the room

And wear his tusk around your neck as a trophy

No one ever calls you out on your BS

You are immune to feedback

And somehow above criticism

You are perfect

But I have no idea how

Super powers do not exist in you

So how do you continue to save the day

When you are a villain

- **The Man**

ME

Front And Center

It took me a while to find myself

I was drifting in a place without a clear connection

Led astray by the distractions of society

I continued to outfit myself with masks

Changing from one front to another

Only allowing glimpses of my true self to shine through

I will never hide again

Hide-and-go seek was a game I never excelled in

This world will know me

The real me

The version who laid dormant

Waiting...the me who stalked his prey like a lion

Slowly waiting for the perfect opportunity

To show my ferocity

The wait is over

Behold

I am

D'MARIO DUPREÉ CARTER

- **Me**